HOW TO LIVE
Successfully
AS A
Christian

JAMES OWUSU

FOREWORD BY PROPHET ISAAC ANTO

HOW TO LIVE
Successfully
AS A
Christian

Empowering Revelations For Every Believer...

JAMES OWUSU

DEDICATION

I dedicate this Book to my one and only Hon. Seth Kwame Acheampong, who is the Regional Minister for Eastern Region of Ghana.

ACKNOWLEDGEMENTS

My first and foremost appreciation goes to the Almighty God for being my Source of the Word.

Secondly, I wish to acknowledge my wife Mrs Deborah Owusu and our lovely children Richardson, Juanita, James and Melchizedek for their care, love and support.

To my spiritual father Prophet Issac Anto, I say God bless you for your covering over my life and ministry.

Also to Richmond Kekeli Ahornor for the priceless works you have done for my ministry.

Finally, to my Pastors and members of City of Testimonies, Tema.

CONTENTS

FOREWORD

Prophet James Owusu Afram is my son in the Lord and I have known him for many years.

To live successfully as a Christian is God's own plan for every Christian. God created us in His own image and became poor so that we must become rich.

This book provides guides that will help every Christian to be successful, how to resist the devil and overcome him.

I believe as you read a copy of this book, God will direct your steps into living a successful life.

Amen!

Ptophet Isaac Anto
[General Overseer, Conqueros Chapel International]

INTRODUCTION

You will never walk in your success until you know your enemy is defeated. The starting point of our right success is not one of the defeats but victory. Christ is our victory.

"But thanks be to God who giveth us the victory through our Lord Jesus Christ." (1Cor. 15:57)

We must begin to live a victorious life if we want to be successful as Christians. Defeat and despair are not the kinds of platform from which we can build a strong victorious life. Satan no longer has the power or authority to defeat the sons and daughters of God's royal family.

However, he doesn't have the ability to deceive the children of God, if they understand who they are in Christ Jesus.

Satan is doing his possible best to derail us so that we cannot walk in our right success. But depending on Jesus Christ is the best solution for you to walk in divine success.

CHAPTER ONE

God Gave Man Dominion

God is self-existent. He is invisible, omnipresent, omnipotent and omniscient. He is three persons in one. The three are God the Father, God the Son and God the Holy Spirit. All the three are one in essence.

God existed at the time when nothing was yet created. But it was His plan to bring creation into being. It was also His plan to have a relationship with creation and be close to it.

He, in other words wanted His creation to be able to relate to Him. But how could the creation relate to its invisible creator if it has no idea as to what He looks like? To solve this question God decided that His Son the second person of the Godhead should take the form of any image that can be revealed to His creation.

This image was to be the direct representation of the Godhead. God brought forth His Son with a specific form. Notice, this took place before anything was created. Colossians 1:15-16 tells us what the image of God brought forth. The Bible says: *"who is the image of the invisible God, the first born of every creature; for by Him were all things created, that are in heaven and that are in earth, visible and invisible, whether they be thrones, dominion or principalities or powers, all things were created by Him."*

From the above passage, Jesus is said to be the first born of every creature. But that does not mean of every creature. His birth in this relates only to the image He has become.

He had always existed eternally with the Father as God. This birth is not the same as the virgin birth which took place in human history through Mary. The birth under reference is a birth that took place in the spiritual realm before anything was created. This means that the Son of God was born twice.

The Son therefore existed as the image of the invisible God long before he came down to this earth. He was first begotten as the image of the Godhead in the spiritual realm before he was born of Mary about two thousand years ago. In Gen. 1:26 **"God said, let us make man in our own image after our likeness..."** Notice, God did not say images, but image. As we have already noted.

The Bible makes it clear that; Jesus the first to be before any creature is the image of the invisible God. We are created to look like Him. Man is a direct image to Jesus but not the invisible God. Notice; when we refer to Jesus here, we are not referring to Him in terms of His appearance on this earth but rather in the spiritual realm. John 1:18 tells us, *"No man hath seen God at any time; the only begotten Son which is in the bosom of the Father, He hath declared Him."* In John 6:46, Jesus Himself said **"Not that any man hath seen the Father, save he which is of God, he hath seen the father."** Jesus is saying here that He is the only one who has seen the father. No one else has seen the father.

God gave the Son authority when He became the son of man. In John 5:26, 27 **"For as the Father hath life in himself; and hath given him authority to execute judgment also, because he is the son of man."**

Jesus received authority from His Father, because He has become the son of man. Being the son of man, He must have dominion over the earth. So when God created the son of man, He created Him to have dominion over everything that moves upon the earth.

Note that, we were created in the image of Jesus in the spiritual realm. And when Jesus was coming to the earth, His Father gave Him authority over everything on this earth. So man must also have dominion over the earth.

The Lord made man for a divine purpose. Gen. 1:26 tells us; *"and God said, let us make man in our own image after our likeness: and let them have dominion over the fishes on the sea, and over the foul of the air and over the cattle and over every creeping thing that creepeth upon the earth."*

The whole earth was given over to man's rule. Notice the word **'over'**. This means that man must rule everything on this earth. Man was made for that purpose. God made him the head of chief authority over the earth. David confirms this in the book of Psalms when he spoke of the special position that man has in God's plan.

In Psalm 8:4-6, we read: *"What is man, that thou art mindful of Him? And the son of man, that thou visitest him? For thou hast made him a little lower than the angels and hast crowned him with glory and honor. Thou madest Him to have dominion over the works of thy hands; thou hast put all things under His feet."*

Man was created to exercise dominion over all the works of God's hand. He was to rule it all, be head of it all. God made man with intent and for that purpose. In the New Testament, the idea is taken still further.

In Hebrews 2:6-8 we read: *"But one in a certain place testified; saying, what is man that thou art mindful of him? Or the son of man, that thou visitest him? Thou madest him a little lower than the angels: thou crowndest him with glory and honor and didst set him over the works of thy hands. Thou hast put all things in subjection under his feet. For in that, put all in subjection under him. He left nothing that is not put under him. But now we see not yet all the things put under him."*

Nothing has been left outside of the man's dominion who walks in right fellowship and relationship.

God Will Not Change His Mind

The calling to exercise authority will not be taken from man as long as man would maintain the image and likeness of Jesus Christ.

God will not change His mind about His callings. They are without repentance. God will not reverse direction. The Bible says in Rom. 11:29 that, *"For the gifts and calling of God are without repentance."*

This means that God will not change His mind about giving man the dominion. The Greek word for repentance is **"METANOIA"**. It means to have a change of mind. Moses said these words in Num. 23:19. *"God is not a man that he should lie, neither the son of man that He should repent; hath he said and shall he not make it good?"*

God made man and gave him authority and dominion over all the earth. It was a commitment that he was bound to honor for all time and eternity.

He will not change His mind. His purpose for man from the very beginning will forever stay the same. The man in Jesus' image and likeness has divine and royal destiny to exercise dominion and authority in this world. He is to be the head of it all.

Man Lost Dominion To Satan

We know from Gen. 3 that Satan came into the Garden of Eden and by deceiving Eve, gained access to Adam. Apostle Paul tells us in 1Tim. 2:14 that, **"and Adam was not deceived, but the woman being deceived was in the transgression."**

Clearly, Adam was not present while the serpent was talking to the woman. Obviously the serpent and Eve had the dialogue at the absence of Adam. After the serpent had beguiled Eve, Adam came on the scene and realized what he had done. Therefore, he partook of the forbidden fruit with her for several reasons.

In Rom. 5:12, 14, 17, death ruled as king by one man. That one by whom death reigned was the devil. In Heb. 2:14 we read; *'For as much then as the children are partakers of flesh and blood, he also Himself likewise took part of the same, that through death he might destroy him that had the power of the death that is the devil'.*

From this verse, when Adam and Eve disobeyed God, Satan received power over man and brought death. Man came under the dominion of Satan.

In Rom. 6:16 we read: *"know ye not, that to whom ye yield yourselves servants to obey, his servants ye are whom, ye obey whether of sin unto death or of obedience unto righteousness?"*

Adam and Eve lost the right to rule. Satan took over that authority and power and held it fast.

Satan Ruled Through Dominion of Death

Adam had everlasting life as long as he obeyed God. In contrast, when Adam sinned and caused death to pass upon all man, Satan ruled by becoming the channel for the dominion of death.

The devil used this dominion to intimidate mankind. When man sinned, the image and likeness of God was ruined and his relationship with God was broken and lastly, man gave up his headship.

The Sad Result of Man

Sad and tragic things happened as a result of their doubt and disobedience:

- **Lost the covering and authority of God:** they came out of the covering and authority of God and the image of God was marred.
- **Lost the right to rule:** They lost their right therefore to rule over God's creation.
- **Came under a new authority:** They then came under the authority of Satan himself. The devil had taken over the dominion of the earth as he had desired. He had won not by force but by deception. The right to rule over god's creation had shifted from man to the serpent (the devil himself).

Tempting Jesus Proved Satan's Dominion

The devil tempted Jesus by offering him kingship and reign over the earth without going to the cross.

In Matt. 4:8 we read: *'again, the devil taketh him all the kingdom of the world and the glory of them'. And said unto him, "all these things will I give thee, if thou wilt fall down and worship me'.*

At that time, Satan had kingdoms and their glory to offer Jesus. The devil promised them to Jesus on one condition that Jesus would bow down and worship him. The act of falling down and worshipping the devil would be an acknowledgement of Satan's right to rule. As an obedient son of Man, Jesus had to totally rely upon the higher and greater authority of God's word and God's spirit to overcome the temptation.

These are the same resources calculated to you and me. Jesus thereby overcame that temptation and became an example for us.

God Planned To Restore Dominion

Satan not only deceived others but also was under a deception himself. He thought he was right when he was wrong. He really believed he had won victory over both God and man. There was however, an aspect of God's nature he knew about. It is called **"Grace"**. It is based on an unselfish love that seeks to redeem that which is of value.

In the case of man's life the price would be the death of another one called **"the son of Man"**. I believe Satan had not counted on God going so far as to give His only begotten son, Jesus for fallen man. The gist had been given even before man had been created. The Bible says in Rev. 13:8 *"and all that dwell upon the earth shall worship him beast/devil whose names are not written in the book of life of the lamb slain from the foundation of the world."*

This means that, God in His foreknowledge saw that man would sin and need a saviour. So Jesus was chosen for this purpose before man was created. In Peter 1:18-20, we read: *"for as much as ye know that ye were not redeemed with corruptible things as silver and gold from your main conversation received by tradition from your Fathers: but with the precious blood of Christ of a lamb without blemish and without spot; who verily was foreordained before the foundation of the world, but was manifest in these lost times for you"*.

When man fell, God did not change His mind about His plan for a beloved and royal family. It was still His purpose to fill the whole earth with sons and daughters whose lives would reflect the beauty of their God.

Through their love and obedience, the glory of God's kingdom would yet cover the whole earth as the waters covers the sea. Yes, the scepter would again return to the hand of man.

The Promised Seed

As soon as man sinned and fell from his place of royal authority, God's plan of redemption was set in motion. It is of some interest that this plan was first revealed to Satan himself. From the record it would appear that Adam and Eve were also there. The Lord however, spoke directly to the serpent in Gen. 3:14-15. *"and the lord God said unto the serpent, because thou has done this, thou are cursed above all cattle and above every beast of the field; upon thy belly shalt thou go, and dust shalt thou eat all the days of thy life. And I will put enmity between thee and the woman and between their seed and her seed; it shall bruise thy head and thou shall bruise his head."*

The seed of the woman refers to the family line from which Jesus would come in His humanity. The phrase **"bruise your head"** has an added meaning of great importance to our theme on authority.

The term head includes the thought of headship or governmental authority. Now a crushed head is fatal, but a bruised heel is temporary. On the cross Christ crushed the head of Satan and stripped him of all his authority.

Christ's injury was temporary. He rose from the dead three days later. There is another truth to consider here also. There is enmity between the seed of the woman and of the serpent. The seed of the serpent are demons, fallen angels and all follow Satan.

The righteous will also gain a personal victory over the devil and crush the head of the serpent.

The Royal Redeemer

God's Son as the son of Man would regain for the redeemed man, the authority to govern that which he lost through sin. The kingdom of heaven will one day rule the earth through God's sons and daughters.

Jesus our redeemer and brother is the first born of God's glorious family. Through Him we have victory, which will last forever. The restored righteous government through God's royal seed can be traced all through scripture. Gal. 4:4-7, Paul says: *"But when the fullness of the time was come God sent forth His son made of woman, made under the law to redeem them that were under the law that we might receive the adoption of sons. And because ye are sons, God hath sent forth the spirit the spirit of his son unto your heart, crying Abba Father! Where thou art no more a servant, but a son: and if a son there an heir of God through Christ."*

In this passage, Paul is linking the birth of the Lord Jesus Christ to the promised seed in Genesis 3:15. Jesus Christ came to this world born of a woman. He came for the purpose of redeeming mankind and restoring him (man) to a place of authority in the family of God.

Jesus fulfilled the prophecy given to the serpent in the Garden of Eden. When the appointed time came through the cross of Christ, Satan was defeated and dethroned. The authority which he took from the first family has been returned to the redeemed sons and daughters of God.

Satan Tried to Advert the Plan

This truth helps us understand the earthly ministry of Jesus, which the devil first seeks to challenge the source of Jesus' divine authority by questioning his divine Sonship. In Mathew 4:3, we read; ***"...if thou be son of God ..."***

The last temptation however brings the issue of authority and dominion into sharp focus.

"Again the devil taketh him up into an exceeding high mountain and showeth him all the kingdom of the world, and the glory of them: and said unto him, all these things will I give thee, if thou wilt fall down and worship me. Then said Jesus unto him, Get thee hence Satan for it is written, thou shall worship the Lord thy God and him only shall thou serve. Then the devil leaveth him and behold angels came and ministered unto him."

We came under authority of the one we worship. Actually, what we worship becomes our authority. No wonder the devil said to him, **"if you will come under my authority, I will give you rulership over all the kingdom of the earth."** Jesus rebuked the devil and refused to be deceived by him.

Satan Had Authority

Satan actually had dominion and authority over the kingdom of the earth. It was the authority, which he took from Adam when he disobeyed God in the Garden of Eden. When Adam and Eve submitted themselves to the lies to the devil, they came under his authority and lost their authority. It was this authority and dominion which Jesus came to regain for the true worshippers of the true God. God already told Satan of this restoration back in the Garden of Eden. Since that time the devil had sought to destroy the line which that royal seed would come.

Satan Didn't Understand Man's Salvation

While Satan knew his kingdom and power was threatened by Jesus, it is possible he didn't know the method and means Jesus would use to defeat him. Apostle Paul tells us that the plan of man's salvation through the cross was not by the rulers or princes of this world. In 1 Corinthians 2:8 we read:

"Which none of the princes of this world knew; for had they known it they would not have crucified the Lord of Glory."

Jesus was fully aware that He must first suffer before entering into His glory.

Luke 24:26 says, *Jesus Has All Authority And Power.*

After Jesus' resurrection, he plainly revealed the truth in these words; *"All power is given unto me in heaven and in earth … I am with you always, even unto the end of the world, Amen!"* (Mathew 28:18-20)

The word **power** means to rule, to take authority and dominion. If Jesus has all power and authority, it also means the devil has none. Through His death on the cross Jesus dethroned the devil and took away his power of death. Apostle John in his heavenly vision in Revelation 1:17-18, the Bible says: *"And when I saw him, I fell at his feet as dead; And he laid His right hand upon me, saying unto me, fear not; I am the first and the last; I am he that lived and was* *dead and behold, I am alive for evermore, Amen; and have the keys of hell and of death."*

CHAPTER FOUR

Jesus The Right Success

Jesus declare that all power have been given unto Him. And His name is above every name. Without Jesus, there is no right to success. You can be the top but without Jesus, you are not going to experience lasting success. Temporal success, come from Satan and right from time lasting success, come from Jesus Christ only. Apostle John says in John 14:6 *"Jesus saith unto him, I am the way, the truth and the life; no man cometh unto the Father but by me."*

In this message we can clearly see that, Jesus is the way to right and true lasting success. He can bring true success but not false success. He can give us a success which includes life, peace, wealth and joy. When you depend on Satan, he will steal, kill and destroy. But when you depend on Jesus you will get life and have it more abundantly. (See John

10:10). To live under the authority of Jesus Christ, you will be lead to true lasting and divine success.

Jesus the Word of God

Jesus is the word of God. The Bible is God's voice, it is God speaking to us; the sacred scriptures are in fact a revelation from God to man. God has given to man a special, infallible and supernatural revelation, thus the Bible. The Bible was written for all disciple of Jesus Christ for our learning so that through its example and practice, we might have hope. The Bible says in John 8:31 **"Then said Jesus to the Jews which believed on him, if ye continue in my word, then are ye my disciples indeed."**

As we are disciples of Jesus Christ, we must be obedient to the word of God because God speaks to us through the word. Apostle John proved that Jesus was the word. In John 1: 1-3 *"In the beginning was the Word, and the Word was with God, and the Word was God. The same was in the beginning with God. All things were made by him; and without him was not anything made that was made."*

Apostle John was saying that the Word was in the beginning with God. Who is that Word? Jesus was the Word. Apostle John says also in John 1:14 *"And the Word was made flesh and dwelt among us, (and we beheld his glory the glory as of the only begotten son of the Father) full of grace and truth."*

In this passage, Apostle John was saying the Word, which became flesh was Jesus. The meaning of Jesus is Salvation.

As Jesus is the Word (The Bible), and it is the Bible which leads us to Salvation.

Salvation means deliverance from sin and the consequences of sin. Jesus came to deliver us from our sins. By keeping the scriptures, you will also be delivered from sin, to walk uprightly. By this, I trust that you have clearly catch the revelation that the Word becoming flesh was Jesus.

Divine Inspiration

Inspiration is the in breathing of God into man, thus qualifying them to receive and communicate divine truth. It is the Holy Spirit speaking through man to man. It is the work of God through the Spirit in man, enabling them to receive and give forth divine truth without error. According to 2 Timothy 3:16: ***"All scriptures are given by inspiration of God and are profitable for doctrine, for reproof, for correction for instruction in righteousness."***

All scriptures (every single word) is God-breathed or filled with the breath of God. The Bible is the product of the divine breath of the Spirit of God. The same breath that breathed life into the nostrils of Adam also brought life into man who penned the sacred words. The scriptures are not just inspired, they are God-inspired. The Bible is the direct result of the powerful creative breath of God, the same breath that created all the hosts of heaven. (Psalm 33:6).

Depend On the Word

Now we know that Jesus is the Word. The very name of the

Lord Jesus Christ is the Word of God (John 1:1; 1:14) and He is the same yesterday, today and forever. Depending on the word is depending on Jesus. In John 3:36 it reads *"He that believeth on the Son hath everlasting life; and he that believeth not the Son shall not see life; but the wrath of God abideth on him."*

In this passage believing in the son, you will get everlasting life. But not believing in the Son, you will abide with the wrath of God. Believing in the Son will bring the right success to you.

Therefore, if Jesus is the Word, then we must believe the word, which is the Bible and that will bring you into the right true and lasting success. Apostle John said in John 17: 17 *"Sanctify them through thy truth; thy word is truth."*

The word of God is true. Depending on the word of God will bring divine success to you. We know divine success comes from Jesus and if Jesus is the Word, then the Word brings divine success to us. Nothing can give you divine success apart from Jesus. In Jeremiah 17: 17 *"Blessed is the man that trusteth in the Lord and whose hope the Lord is."*

Jeremiah was saying when we trust in the Lord we will be blessed. Well, we cannot see God physically but through His inspiration revealed through men we have come to know His voice. So what Jeremiah wants to tell us is that we should trust in God's word and be blessed; By so doing you attract and activate God's divine blesssings which was promised to our fathers.

What kind of success do you need from God which He cannot do? Paul says in 2 Corinthians 9:8 " *And God is able to make all grace abound toward you; that ye, always having all sufficiency in all things, may abound to every good work.*"

God is able to do all things physically, spiritually and mentally.

CHAPTER FIVE

Living In Your Right Success

J esus does not only have all power and authority, but He has given that power to his disciples. The Bible declares in Luke 10:17-19

"And the seventy returned again with joy saying, Lord even the devils are subject unto? Through thy name. And He said unto them I beheld Satan as lighting fall from heaven. Behold, I give unto your power to tread on serpents and scorpions and over all the power of the enemy and nothing shall be any means hurt you."

Don't retreat, because we are all sons and daughters in the family of God. We have the authority and privilege of Christ's name. You may ask these questions yourselves, why then are so many Christians living defeated lives?

Where is your victory in Christ? The words sound good, but where are the works? The answers can be found in one of Peter's Epistles. Peter's words are very powerful and practical. In 1 Peter 5:8-9, the Bible says;

"Be sober, be vigilant; because your adversary the devil, as a roaring lion, walketh about, seeking whom he may devour, whom resist steadfast in the faith, knowing that the same afflictions are accomplished in your brethren that are in the world."

In this passage, the devil is not a roaring lion. In other words, he is acting like something he is not. Jesus is the real lion. The scriptures refers to Him as **'the Lion of the tribe of Judah'**. (See Revelation 5:5) Because we abide in Him and He is in us, we also share in His **'lion nature'** and through Him we become 'lion-like'. In Proverbs 28:1 the Bible declares *"The wicked flee when no man pursueth; but the righteous are bold as a lion."*

The devil can only have power over our lives if we allow him. He no longer has the authority to control our attitudes and actions for his own purposes. He will however, take as much control as we will let him have. He cannot over power us anymore like he overpowered Adam and Eve in the Garden of Eden. He will seek to deceive us in the same way he tempted them. If we retreat every time the devil roars, we never learn how to stand firm in the faith and resist him. If we never resist the devil, we will never see the tail-end of the devil.

Resist The Devil

To be successful as a Christian, you must resist the devil. The Bible says in James 4:7 *"Submit yourselves therefore to God. Resist the devil and he will flee from you."*

If you resist the devil he will flee from you. But if you however, do not, get to know that, he will destroy your divine success. In John 10:10, the Bible says **"The thief cometh not, but for to steal and to kill and to destroy…"**

In this passage, you can see that, the devil's primary aim is to steal, to kill and to destroy; therefore, we must resist him. The language of the devil is destruction. The Bible says in Exodus 15:9; *"The enemy said, I will overtake, I will divide the spoil; my lust shall be satisfied upon them; I will draw my sword, my hand shall destroy them."*

In this passage, the purpose of the devil is to destroy what God has given unto us, that is why God said we should resist him. In John 10:10, John mentioned to steal, kill and destroy and Exodus 15:9, Moses also mentioned I will pursue, I will overtake and I will divide the spoil.

In these two passages Moses and John mentioned three ways the devil has been working against our lives. These tell us that whenever the devil is coming in our life he comes in three different says. He will try the first one, if he misses then he moves to the second one and then moves to the third one.

The spelling of S-I-N. The word is three letter words. Satan deceived the woman namely, Eve and the spelling is three letter words. Note that, the devil had been coping with what God had been doing.

The personalities of God are in three that is God the Father, God the Son and God the Holy Spirit. In Genesis 1:26, these three personalities operated together. Because the devil doesn't have three personalities, he operates in these three different ways as Moses and John mentioned.

How To Resist The Devil

(1) Stand firm in Faith:

You will ask this question yourself, how can we be a watchful Christian, stand in faith and resist the devil?
Jesus proved it while here on the earth by:
- the authority of God's Word
- the power of God's Spirit

Note that, the devil no longer has dominion. The scepter is now in Jesus' hand. So by the speaking out of our confession of faith **'JUSUS IS LORD'** Satan must bend his knee and bow his head.

(2) Speaking the Word in Faith:

As we submit ourselves and come under the authority of God's Word and God's Spirit that authority comes upon us. We then speak the word as follows:
- To God in Prayer
- In the Confession of our mouth

- To devil in rebuke

The Spirit himself then moves to energize the word and the enemy flees.

(3) **Submit to God:**

We submit ourselves to God by feeding our minds with His word and our hearts with prayer. Negative thoughts come from the enemy and positive thoughts comes from God. To get positive thoughts, you habe to read the scriptures. Paul says in Romans 12:21 ***"overcome evil with good."*** All the time, the devil seeks to give us wrong directions, but we can only resist his wrong directions with the truth and power of God's Word.

(4) **The laugh of Faith:**

We shouldn't underrate the devil's ability because he is smart. Apart from God's Spirit and His Word, we will lose every battle. Satan can out smart us every time if we are ignorant of God's word.

The Bible says that we should always be aware of his clever tricks and schemes (See 2 Corinthians 2:11). Our enemy has a loud roar, and also a big bluff. He will act like he is not hurt and even mock the name of the lord, hoping we will give up. If we respond with the faith we have in God, we press our attacks on him and he will flee in fear. When we are in a position of high authority and the enemy is truly beneath our feet, then we have defeated him. Having faith in Christ gives us authority over the enemy and we will overcome him all the time if our trust is in Him.

(5) Putting Principles Into Practice:

Everything we hear, study and speak the Word of God by faith we get to stand in a favourable position to resist the devil. After all the most important thing is to exercise that faith which we acquire through His word. Putting the our faith into practice will make us dominate the enemy. Otherwise, the enemy will deceive us and cause us to perish.

"Faith rises up and resists, but unbelief gives up and accepts the lies of the enemy." - James Owusu

Overcome the Devil

You cannot live successful as a christian if you do not resist the devil. But before you resist the devil, you must overcome the devil. We overcome the devil through Jesus Christ and we resist the devil through ourselves by the faith we manifest in Christ. Jesus Christ had overcome the devil and charges us to resist the devil and he will flee from us.

Overcome is two words coming together, that 'OVER' and 'COME'. Tribulations will 'come' but overcome the devil. Believers of Jesus Christ are ignorant of the devil who is the greatest enemy of their soul. The Apostle Paul warned God's children not to be ignorant of what they need to know. Being ignorant of the strength and weakness of the devil is tragedy which can be a disaster.

The Bible gives the true children of God every information they needed to know about the greatest enemy of their life thus, the devil. Many of God's children are ignorant of the devil and how he operates because of spiritual laziness as they don't have time to study God's Words. Believers can know and defeat of the devil through our Lord Jesus Christ whiles He can also plunder the stronghold of the devil and set his captives free.

How to Overcome the Devil

(1) The Word of God:

Jesus overcomes the devil with the written Word of God. When Jesus met the devil in the wilderness, he did not argue with him to prove his deity as the Son of God when he questioned him concerning his divined sonship. Jesus quoted the written Word of God to silence his arguments.

Jesus knowing His deity as the Son of God did not have to prove it by any means because He's the eternal Son of God. If Jesus could have obeyed the devil's command to turn the stone to bread, his obedience to the devil's command could have caused Jesus to fall into the same sin which caused Adam and Eve to fall from grace. (See Matthew 4) This is the first recorded victory over the devil with the sword of the Holy Spirit which is the word of God. When He proclaimed the word, it became a spiritual sword which drove the devil out of His presence. You will ask, can I overcome the devil as Jesus did? The answer to this question can be found in the epistle of 1 John 2:14;

"I have written unto you, fathers, because ye have overcome him that is from the beginning. I have written unto you,

young men, because ye are strong and the word of God abideth in you and ye have overcome the wicked one."

When the word of God abides in you, then you can overcome the devil because it will help you not to sin against God (See Psalm 119:11). The word of God can guide your feet in your spiritual walk with God as a lamp, as light guides men to walk in darkness without stumbling. It will counsel and teach thy mouth to speak the word of God. (See Psalm 37:30-31; Proverbs 6:20-21). It will protect and direct the course of thy living (See Proverbs 6:20-23). It will make the child of God spiritually strong and give him power needed to overcome the devil (See 1 John 2:14).

The Word of God abiding in the child of God will helps us to live and work in the spirit thereby empowering us to tread over serpents and scorpions and over all power of the devil and nothing shall by any means hurt us.

The Holy Spirit can wield the spiritual sword of God's word and empower the soldier of Christ to overcome the devil and his demons in spiritual warfare. Take hold of God's word. Keep it in your heart as your hidden treasure. Digest it in your mind by meditating on it day and night.

Release your faith in God's words by proclaiming it with your mouth daily. Believe with all your heart that the Word of God which you proclaim out of your month will not come back to you void, but it shall accomplish the purpose for which it was sent and prosper.

(2) The Power of Prayer:

Jesus overcomes the devil through the power of prayer. In the garden of Gethsemane, Jesus fought His final battle with the devil on His way to the cross. When Jesus knew that the time for His crucifixion was at hand, He withdrew Himself with His disciples into the garden of Gethsemane. Where He fought His final battle with the devil and overcome him through the power of prayer (See Mark 14:32-42). The child of God can overcome the devil through the power of prayer as Jesus did in the garden of Gethsemane.

Your garden of Gethsemane is where you stand and pray or go on your knees and pray. The secret of spiritual strength to endure trials and temptations is the believer's ability to pray. Your spiritual strength is the intensity of your prayer life. Spiritual strength is the ability to suffer long with a rejoicing spirit.

The ability not only to pray but also to be able to rejoice in times of trials, troubles, persecutions and hardship is an indication of spiritual strength. An example of rejoicing in a time of trial could be seen in the lives of the believer in the book of Acts 5:40-41. The spiritual strength of the believer of Jesus Christ is the frequency of his prayer life especially in times of great affliction and prosperity.

Many believers find it extremely difficult to pray effectively when they have everything they need around them without any sweat. Prosperity then becomes their dependence instead of God. They no longer take time seeking God to know what to do with the wealth He has given them.

They will just take some bunch of money to do whatever they think is right in their own eyes for God and ask Him to bless it. Others also find it extremely difficult to persevere in prayer in time of great allocations. They spend much time complaining, Jesus did not overcome the devil on his cross for Himself but rather for the benefit of the fallen men to be redeemed. The believer has already overcome the devil and sin through the finished work of Jesus Christ on the cross. Murmuring and spending less time in prayer before God can put a believer unto a life of affliction. The believer is then spiritually weak and there the devil afflicts the believer with problems. A believer, who is spiritually weak, needs to wait upon the Lord and seek Him until He renews his strength. Divine strength from God is what gives us power to mount on wings like an eagle.

Apostle Paul and Silas were symbols of spiritual strength as they weathered through the storms of persecution by their exhibition of prayer and praise after severe lashes. (See Acts 16:23-25) A fervent prayer life in times of temptation is an indication of a believer's spiritual strength even as we can see by the examples of Apostle Paul, Silas, Peter, John and others. Because of their spiritual strength, these men of God were able to mount on wings like eagles by weathering the storms of persecutions, trials and tribulations without fainting or becoming weary. (See Isaiah 40:29-31)

(3) The Crucifixion of Jesus Christ on the Cross:

The Crucifixion of Jesus Christ on His cross was a physical display of His victory over the devil. If the devil knew that the Crucifixion of Jesus would be the destruction of his kingdom, he wouldn't have influenced Judas Iscariot and the religious leaders to make a plot to crucify Him.

Apostle Paul unveiling the mystery of the Crucifixion of Christ described the overwhelming humiliation and defeat that was brought to the devil and his kingdom after the resurrection of Jesus. In the book of Colossians 2:14-15; *"Blotting out the handwriting of ordinances that was against us, which was contrary to us an took it out of the way, nailing it to his cross; And having spoiled principalities and power he made a show of them openly, triumphing over them in it."*

By His Crucifixion on the cross, the power of sin and of the devil was destroyed. The believer of Jesus Christ can overcome the devil through the cross and partaking in the understanding of the purpose of His Crucifixion on the cross. Most believers, who do understand the purpose of Christ's Crucifixion on the cross, enjoy the benefits of the cross.

Lack of knowledge of the truth about Christ's Crucifixion on the cross will cause you to be religious by partaking in the ceremony of baptism in water without experiencing the reality of the practical application of the cross in your life.

Because of this, many believers of Jesus Christ lack the

personal experience of what it means to be crucified with Christ. The secret of the believer's joint victory with Christ through the cross in the realization of His joint crucifixion, burial and resurrection and be seated at the right hand of God the Father. Knowing this will help you to seek for the true experience and reality of your joint death and crucifixion with Christ in order to reap all the benefits of the cross.

Lack of knowledge will cause you to go through all the religious formalities without the practical experience which is the reality of the cross in the believer's spiritual life. In Romans 6:6-7, the Bible says *"Knowing this, that our old man is crucified with him, that the body of sin might be destroyed, that henceforth we should not serve sin. For he that is dead is freed from sin."*

When Christ hanged on the cross, He died with everything that had anything to do with the Adamic race. Adamic nature transplanted into the fallen man because of sin was destroyed. The divine act of the crucifixion, burial and resurrection with Christ is the act of baptism in water.

Baptism in water is a symbol of what has truly taken place spiritually in the believer's life, but not religious rituals. Undergoing religious rituals of the baptism in water without experiencing the reality of the death, burial and resurrection with Christ makes believers religious.

That is the main reason why Apostle Paul prayed that he

may truly experience the reality of this divine act of His dead, burial and resurrection with Christ (See Phil 3:10-11)

(4) **The Shed Blood on the Cross:**

Jesus overcomes the devil by his shedding of blood on the cross. The cross is the only way through which God could redeem the world from the dominion of the devil and sin after the fall of man.

This was ordained through the shedding of the blood of Jesus Christ. This is the blood that was shed before the foundation of the world. (Revelation 13:8; 1 Peter 1:19-20)

The deliverance power of the shedding blood of Jesus Christ can be perfectly understood by relating it to the Old Testament when the blood of sheeps and calves were applied which were shadows of the sinner is the blood of Christ which is the reality.

Under the new covenant, the shedding of the blood of Jesus of Christ did not cover the sins of the sinner as the blood of sheep and calves did under the old covenant.

Rather the shedding blood of Christ takes away the sins of the sinner the moment he chooses to believe in the death, burial and resurrection of Christ.

Once the shedding blood of Jesus Christ takes away the sins of the sinners, he has been delivered from the bondage of his sins.

We can now enjoy freedom from the dominion of sin because the power of sin which held us as prisoners of Satan has been destroyed and our soul has escaped out of the snare of the fowler. Our relationship with God has been restored so that we can now enter into the presence of God through faith in the shedding blood lf Jesus Christ.

The shedding of the blood of Jesus has overcome the devil because it has destroyed the power of sin through the devil which held the sinner in a prison.

Prophet Zachariah foresaw this when he wrote by the inspiration of God concerning the redemption power of the blood of Jesus Christ, the book of Zachariah 9:11, '*As for thee also, by the blood of thy covenant, I have sent forth thy prisoners out of the pit wherein no water is*'.

The shedding blood of Jesus Christ overcomes the devil because God through its power has redeemed mankind from the bandage of sin. The shedding blood of Jesus Christ is the believer's answer to the devil's accusations and condemnation.

The power of sin which brought spiritual death to mankind has been destroyed by the shedding blood of Jesus Christ. It's the complete defeat of the devil and the believer's victory over sin.

The devil knows this and every believer of Jesus Christ who knows this truth well and applies it to himself can never be held hostage as his prisoner. The believer can overcome the devil through the shed blood of Jesus Christ.

We can also can overcome by believing in Jesus Christ as a partaker of His victory over the devil through His shed blood. The victory of the believer over the devil through the blood of Christ takes place during the new birth where the blood takes away every stain of sin from the believer and makes him a new creation.

On that day of salvation where the sinner repents and confesses Jesus as His personal Savior and Lord, the yoke of sin through which the devil held the sinner as his captive is destroyed and the sinner is now free from the dominion of the devil.

In revelation 12:11, the Bible says: *"And they overcame him (Satan) by the blood of the Lamb and by the word of their testimony; and they loved not their lives unto the death."*

This is the first phase of the believer's victory over the devil through the shedding blood of Christ. The second victory of the believer over the devil through the shedding blood of Christ comes on right after his new birth in Christ.

Even though he has been delivered from the bondage of sin, yet he may fall into sin. This is where the devil will take the new believer on by accusing and condemning him by calling him a sinner. A sinner is anyone who has not yet repented, believed and confessed Jesus Christ as Personal

Savior and Lord.

Anyone who has done this is no more a sinner. But if after doing this and he falls into sin, that doesn't make him the same old sinner because he has been washed in the precious blood of Jesus Christ, but he has only been stained with sin. New believers get confused and condemn themselves because they don't have knowledge of the truth. If we know the truth, we won't condemn ourselves but instead, we will humbly confess our sins with repentant heart and mind and the blood of Jesus Christ will once again cleanse all form of unrighteousness. The Bible says in 1 John 2:1-2; *"My little children, these things write I unto you that ye sin not. And if any man sin, we have advocate with the father, Jesus Christ the righteous, and he is the propitiation for our sins; and not for ours only, but also for the sins of the whole world."*

Also the Bible says in 1 John 1:9; *"if we confess our sins, he is faithful and just to forgive us our sins and to cleanse us from all unrighteousness."*

The complete eradication of our sins and continual cleansing of the blood of Jesus Christ is the belier's victory over the devil. We can also apply the blood of Jesus by faith for divine protection of ourselves and properties.

If the believer learns to apply the blood of Jesus for personal forgiveness, deliverance, protection, progressive sanctification and purification, he is always in the safe hands of God's protection and has overcome the devil through the shedding blood of Jesus Christ.

(5) The Resurrection from the Dead:

The complete victory of Christ and the final defeat over the devil was the resurrection from the dead. By His resurrection from the dead, He displayed His victory over the devil who had since the fall of mankind taken him as his prisoner of war through the bondage of sin and death. In Hebrews 2:14, the Bible says: *"Forasmuch then as the children are partakers of flesh and blood, he also himself likewise took part of the same; that through death he might destroy him that had the power of death that is the devil."*

From the passage, it explains how Jesus partook in mankind's death, so that through His physical resurrection from death, He could deliver those who through the fear of death became the prisoners of Satan.

The sting of death which throughout the centuries had held mankind dead spiritually and physically without any hope of physical resurrection from the dead, was destroyed through the physical resurrection of Jesus Christ Himself.

His physical resurrection from the dead was His assurance to His followers that He had conquered death spiritually and physically. Before His death, He declared that He had power to lay down His own life and take it back through His resurrection from the death.

Death has been swallowed up in victory by the physical resurrection of Jesus Christ. True to His words, He laid down His own life just to partake in mankind's death spiritually so that through His death, He could collect the keys of death and hell. Jesus reveals Himself to Apostle John in Revelation 1:18 saying: *"I am He that liveth and was dead, and behold I am alive for evermore, Amen; and have the keys of hell and death."*

These precious words of our Lord Jesus Christ clearly explains that He did not partake in mankind's death just of the pleasure of it but that through the partaking of mankind's death, He might have the opportunity to overpower the devil to collect the keys of death and hell before His resurrection from the dead. A believer can overcome the devil through our identification and union with the resurrection of Christ. Jesus did not resurrect just to prove to the devil that He had power over him because He created the devil.

He partook in the nature of man so that He could identify Himself with mankind and save him. He chose to live the lowest life on earth so that He could understand even the smallest problems of mankind.

He laid down His life to be crucified on the cross so that He could destroy him who had power of sin and death. He died so that He could destroy the power of death by His resurrection from the dead.

He did not only resurrect from the dead but He also triumph over the devil and all his agents. He resurrected from the dead, took the keys of death and hell so that He might have the power to resurrect mankind from the dead to judge them. The bible says in John 5:28-29, *"Marvel not at this; for the hour is coming; in which all that are in the graces shall hear his voice; And shall come forth; they that have good, unto the resurrection of life; and they that have done evil unto the resurrection of damnation."*

Through His resurrection, Jesus has purchased for mankind the resurrection from the dead. He has delivered those who believe in Him from the fear of death and judgment unto condemnation. Jesus conquered death and hell for the benefit of all mankind especially those who may believe in him.

The believer's faith in the death, burial and resurrection of Christ should give him personal assurance of the blessed hope of his bodily resurrect on from the dead if he dies before the coming of Christ. 1Thessalonians 4:13-14, the Bible says:

'But I would not have you to be ignorant, brethren, concerning them which are asleep, that ye sorrow not, even as others which have no hope. For if we believe that Jesus died and rose again, even so them, also which sleeps in Jesus will God bring with him.'

Everything Jesus did right from His birth, to His resurrection and ascension was for the benefit of mankind. Even the Bible declares that, those who believe in Him are seated with Him at the right hand of God the Father in Heaven (Ephesians 2:6). The bodily resurrection of Jesus Christ from the dead is a victory banner of the believer over the devil, sin, death and hell.

(6) Spiritual Resurrection of a Believer:

Spiritual resurrection is simply the quickening of our human spirits by the Holy Spirit to give us life. This takes place during the new birth when the sinner believes and confesses Jesus Christ as his personal Savior and Lord.

The blood of Jesus Christ cleanses us from all sins and then the Holy Spirit comes to reside in us by resurrecting our human spirit.

His operation takes place in our hearts and our human spirit which was dead and isolated from God because of sin has been resurrected by God to enjoy the fellowship of the Holy Spirit. In Ephesians 5:14, the Bible says:

"Wherefore he saith, awake thou that sleepest and arise from the dead and Christ shall give thee light."

Once his human spirit has been resurrected from, the dead by the Holy Spirit, the believer will now begin to experience the resurrected life of Christ.

This is a new life springing from the regenerating power of

the Holy Spirit flowing through the believer's human spirit to manifest itself through the production of the fruits and gifts of the Holy Spirit.

This is learning, to live, walk and to be led by the Holy Spirit. This is supernatural life which one can live victoriously by overcoming temptations, trials, persecutions, adversities, tribulations, hardships and every fiery dart of the devil.

This is the abundant life which Jesus promised those who will believe in Him if they allow the Holy Spirit to work through them as the sanctified vessels of God prepared for the master's use.

Always Remember!

You are a son or daughter in the beloved family of God. The Lord loves you and desires you to take the scepter in your hands and confess the liberty which is rightfully yours. You no longer need to shrink back in fear or hang yourself in shame.

Jesus came to set you free and He whom the Son set free is free indeed. Amen!!!

THE AUTHOR

James Owusu is a Christian statesman, advisor to leaders, father to many, and a mentor to a number of Christian leaders who has submitted to his prophetic grace.

He is the President of James Owusu Ministrries; a ministry which seeks to cause liberation to people from all walks of life, discover and direct destinies through the prophetic ministry.

He is happily married to the Mrs. Deborah Owusu and they are blessed with four wonderful children.

Get Connected

- James Owusu
- Prophet James Owusu
- Prophet James Owusu
- +233 244087189
- jamesowusuministries@gmail.com